I AM
Choosing Who I Am

A Self-Discovery & Empowerment Book for Growing Learners

Dr. Tache' Vereen

ISBN: 979-8-9993418-5-3

Published by DOC with TV LLC

Book Cover & Layout Design: Abu Bakar Javed

TABLE OF CONTENTS

A Message to You

Hello,

This is not just a book—it's a journey of learning, reflection, and choosing who you are.

As you move through these pages, you'll be invited to think about your thoughts, your actions, your strengths, and the kind of person you want to become. Each chapter will help you better understand yourself and the choices that shape your identity.

You are unique, and the choices you make play an important role in who you are becoming. Your growth, your experiences, and even your challenges can help shape your character in meaningful ways.

As you read, take your time. Be honest with yourself. There is no need to compare your journey to anyone else's—this is your process.

Use this book as a space to reflect, write, and explore your ideas. And if you need guidance, don't hesitate to talk with a parent, teacher, or trusted adult who can support you along the way.

Most importantly, remember that who you are becoming is something you have a role in shaping.

This journey is yours—own it.

— Welcome to your journey of choosing who you are.

CHAPTER 1

A Moment in Gym Class

When I was in elementary school, I remember sitting in gym class while everyone else played.

The gym was loud.

Shoes squeaked on the floor in a rhythm like an old door shutting.

Hockey sticks slammed and scratched across the floor as kids played indoor hockey.

The puck sounded like it wished it wasn't a hockey puck because the kids were trying so hard to win.

All my friends were running, laughing, and playing.

And there I was, sitting at the other end of the gym with my science and invention book in my hands.

I wasn't trying to skip class. I just loved learning. I was so excited to go to the gym that day—not to play—but because I had my book, and I knew I could take a quiet seat and read. In my other classes, I rarely got that chance because I followed directions and loved to learn.

Even at home, I would carry these books in my backpack so I could read them on the bus or whenever I had a free moment. They were fascinating—full of ideas about how things are made. Making paper caught my attention the most.

I started wondering: Had anyone thought of this before? Could I actually make the paper myself? How much could I make? How much could I sell? Who would want to buy it?

I had a whole plan in my head. I remembered seeing someone run a lemonade stand and thought, Maybe I could have a paper stand. I even imagined myself on a Saturday in my neighborhood, selling the paper I made. I could see my friends and neighbors getting excited about what I created and wanting to buy some to use for homework or to write their own thoughts.

As I read and imagined, the noisy gym faded away. Even though no one asked what I was reading or what I was thinking, it felt like I was invisible—but my mind was anything but quiet. It was racing with ideas.

That day, I realized something important: I didn't need everyone to see me. I needed to see myself.

I needed to believe in my ideas. I needed to believe in my creativity. Even though no one noticed me, I realized how awesome I could be—someone with big ideas worth exploring.

I wanted someone to notice, maybe even call my mom to say, You have a creator in the making. But even if no one did, I knew one thing for sure:

I had to see myself.

I had to honor my dreams—even if I was the first one to believe in them.

SCHOOL GYM
PASS!
LOOK OUT!
HAHA!
NOISE!
PLAY!
LET'S GO!
HOME 09
GUEST 07
03:17
One idea... can change everything.
My Paper Stand
Making the Paper
Inspiring Others
While the wor
was loud...
my dream
were loud t
BIG IDEAS
Start Small
INVENTIONS
GREAT IDEAS
WOMEN LEADERS
CREATIVITY
THE WORLD OF BUSINESS

Think About It...

Have you ever had a moment when you were so focused on something you love that you didn't notice anything else around you? What were you doing, and why was it important to you?

Use these words to discover and describe who you are. Choose the ones that feel most like you.

creative	imaginative
confident	determined
curious	bold
independent	innovative
focused	self-aware

____

____

____

____

____

____

____

Say Your 'I Am' Statement With Confidence And Own It.

I AM

*Keep believing in yourself,
even when it feels like no
one else does!*

CHAPTER 2

Words That Stick

Words can be powerful. We often hear the saying, "Sticks and stones may break my bones, but words will never hurt me." But for many people, including me, that wasn't true.

I remember a time when my mother took me to the hairdresser to get my hair done. I was supposed to take better care of my hair, but I didn't always follow my mom's instructions.

When we went to the salon, the hairdresser told my mom that my hair was very damaged and needed to be cut. I was devastated. I didn't want my hair cut short, but it had to be done.

The next day when I went to school, some of my classmates noticed my haircut right away. They laughed and called me "bald-headed." Everyone around them laughed too.

I laughed along with them, pretending it didn't bother me.

But inside, their words hurt. I felt embarrassed and wished I could disappear.

I remember wishing I had listened to my mom. I also wished my classmates had chosen kinder words.

That moment stayed with me.

Later, I remembered something else from my childhood.

There was a boy in my class who wore the same pair of sneakers every day during fifth grade. The sneakers were worn and dirty. When he walked by, some of my friends would laugh.

Sometimes I laughed too.

But I noticed something about him. He would lower his head and walk a little faster, as if he wanted to disappear.

Deep down, I knew he couldn't help it. His parents were probably doing the best they could. I understood that feeling because there were things other kids had that my mom couldn't afford to buy for me.

At that moment, I realized something important—words don't just get said… they stay.

Words have weight.

They can make someone feel small, embarrassed, or ashamed. But words can also lift people up and make them feel seen and valued.

The words we choose matter.

Instead of bringing rain into someone's day, we can choose to be sunshine. We can choose to speak encouragement, kindness, and understanding.

A few kind words might seem small, but they can stay with someone long after the moment is over.

CLASSROOM

Think About It...

Can you remember a time when someone's words hurt you? How did it make you feel?

Use these words to discover and describe who you are. Choose the ones that feel most like you.

kind-hearted	considerate
compassionate	encouraging
respectful	supportive
empathetic	gentle
mindful	responsible

____

____

____

____

____

____

Say Your 'I Am' Statement With Confidence And Own It.

I AM ______________________

The words we choose matter. Instead of bringing rain into someone's day, we can choose to be sunshine.

CHAPTER 3

I Watch and I Learn

When I was growing up, there was a neighbor who felt like a grandfather to all the kids in our neighborhood. He wasn't my grandparent, but he treated every one of us like family.

Whenever he saw us, he would stop and greet us with a smile. He told stories about his life, but the thing I remember most is that he listened—really listened—to everything we had to say. He never hurried us or acted annoyed when we asked questions, no matter how small or silly they seemed.

Sometimes, he invited us to church. He even asked our parents if we could ride with him, and on some days, the church van came through our street to make sure we could go. Watching him, I realized that one person's choices can influence many children.

It wasn't just the big gestures. Even little things mattered. He would always have candy and popsicles for us, but he made sure to ask our parents first if it was okay for us to have them. He would sit and read us stories from the Bible, and we would be completely engaged because he was such a wonderful storyteller. During our relay races, he would serve as the judge so no one would fight about who won. He cared about our friendships, and it showed in everything he did.

Seeing how he treated us made me feel noticed and cared for. He remembered what we loved, like candy and popsicles. He cared enough about our fun and friendships to step in when he was needed. Watching him made us want to do the same for each other. We even learned to pick a judge when he wasn't around, realizing that we needed fairness and care just like he showed us.

I also noticed how he watched us closely during the races. Sometimes I wanted to be the judge too, and my friends did as well. We were learning by example—seeing how he stayed patient, kind, and thoughtful made us want to do the same. His attentiveness inspired us all. When he wasn't around, we would ask, "Who is going to be the neighbor today?" and everyone would raise their hands to take on the role.

When he walked into the neighborhood, we would all run up to him, patiently waiting for him to say each of our names individually. It amazed us that he remembered all of our names—it made each of us feel special and seen. That simple act of remembering taught me that paying attention to others is powerful.

That neighbor taught me something important: we are always learning from the people around us. Kids notice how adults act, how they talk, and how they treat others—even when adults don't think anyone is watching. I realized that one person's example can make a difference. Watching him made me want to be patient, kind, and thoughtful too.

So, when you see someone helping, being patient, or showing care, pay attention. You are learning from them—and one day, someone might be watching and learning from you too.

Think About It...

Who do you watch? What do you notice about how they act? How can the way you act teach others too?

Use these words to discover and describe who you are. Choose the ones that feel most like you.

observant	honest
attentive	respectful
thoughtful	responsible
patient	wise
fair	intentional

____

____

____

____

____

____

Say Your 'I Am' Statement With Confidence And Own It.

I AM

Watching him made me want to be patient, kind, and thoughtful too.

CHAPTER 4

The People Who Show Up

I remember a time when I was in my early teenage years, and I loved hanging out with my friends. We would go to the mall, walk through the stores, laugh, and just enjoy being kids. We would leave home around 11 a.m. and not return until later that afternoon. What a time!

But during that season, my mind was often focused on the boys around me. My mother began to notice, and she became concerned. She didn't want me to make some of the same choices she had made as a young teen. She wanted to protect me.

So she did something I didn't expect.

She called a few of my older cousins and my aunt, and they all came together. We sat around the table, and one by one, they began to talk to me. They told me there was nothing wrong with liking boys, but they also said I seemed too focused on it. They were all concerned about me.

At first, I felt like they were trying to control me. I didn't understand why so many people needed to talk to me at once. But as I sat there and listened, something began to change.

I started to hear more than just their words—I heard their hearts. I heard their concern for my life. I heard their love for me. And in that moment, I realized something I hadn't seen before.

They weren't trying to control me. They were trying to help me.

My mother recognized that I might be going down a path that could have changed my future. She also realized she couldn't do it alone. So she asked for help. She knew that maybe I would listen if the message came from others too—and she was right.

That day, I felt seen.

That day, I felt cared for.

That day, I understood love in a different way.

Looking back, I am so grateful. Because if they hadn't stepped in, I might have made choices that could have slowed me down or taken me off track.

That experience taught me something important: We all need people in our lives who will show up for us.

Sometimes, it may feel like you are alone—but don't stay in that feeling. Look around. There are people who care about you. There are people who want to see you do well.

Support doesn't always look the same. It might be your parent, your teacher, your neighbor, or a mentor.

And sometimes, the people who show up won't come with loud voices or big announcements.

Sometimes, they show up with a conversation.

Sometimes, they show up with guidance.

Sometimes, they show up with love.

I didn't always recognize how my mother was showing up for me. She had been talking to me all along, but I wasn't really listening.

But that day, when she brought others around me, I finally saw her heart. I saw how much she loved me. I saw that I wasn't alone.

So remember this:

It's okay to need people.

It's okay to accept help.

Let people show up for you. Let them care for you.

And one day, you will be the person who shows up for someone else.

Think About It...

Have you ever had someone step in to help you, even when you didn't realize you needed it? What happened?

____

____

____

____

____

____

____

____

____

____

____

Use these words to discover and describe who you are. Choose the ones that feel most like you.

supported	encouraged
valued	guided
loved	strong
grateful	secure
connected	appreciative

____

____

____

____

____

____

Say Your 'I Am' Statement With Confidence And Own It.

I AM _______________________________________

"

Sometimes, the people who show up don't come with loud voices—they show up with love.

CHAPTER 5

Being Uniquely You

When I was younger, I was very skinny. Sometimes, the other kids would call me "sticks and bones." It made me feel embarrassed. I didn't understand why they couldn't see that everyone is different. I just wanted to fit in and be like everyone else.

On hot days, I didn't wear layers, but on cold days I would. Layers made me feel bigger, but they also made playing outside harder. Running around felt slow and heavy. I tried to eat more to gain weight, but my body just wouldn't change the way I wanted. I wondered if I would ever look like the other kids.

My mom always encouraged me. She told me I was beautiful and that I could be a model. Her words made me feel seen and special. But she didn't stop there—she showed me how much she believed in me by bringing me to modeling events. I remember seeing girls and boys of all shapes and sizes, and for the first time, I realized that I could shine just as I was.

Some friends noticed that I loved reading science books and learning how to create new things. They would ask me about what I was reading, and I would tell them my plans. They thought it was amazing. For the first time, I felt like someone really saw me—not just my body, but my ideas, my creativity, and my mind.

I also had a teacher who told me I would make a good news caster. At the time, I couldn't picture myself on TV, but her words encouraged me. Slowly, I began to see that my differences were part of what made me strong. My love for reading, my creativity, and even my skinny body were all pieces of what made me unique.

One day, I decided to put what I had learned from my science books into action. I made my own paper and sold it to my friends. Seeing their amazed faces was priceless! I felt proud and excited. In that moment, I realized I was smart, creative, and capable. Being different wasn't something to hide—it was something to celebrate.

I began to understand something very important: it's okay to just be yourself. Everyone has different strengths. Maybe you are a fast runner, a careful listener, a talented artist, or a kind friend. Whatever it is, it makes you special. And when you see someone else being different, celebrate them too. Everyone deserves to feel like they belong.

No matter what anyone says, remember: you are a gift. You don't have to be like anyone else. You don't have to try to fit in. Appreciate your strengths. Celebrate your differences. Be yourself—because this world needs you to be you.

THEN
I'm not good enough... I don't fit in... Why do they judge me?
X Overlooked
X Doubtful
X Trying to be accepted
X Living in fear of judgment
not enough too quiet not pretty not confident
VS.
I am enough
I am worthy
I am becoming everything I dreamed of.
NOW
DETERMINATION DISCIPLINE PURPOSE
CONFIDENCE FOCUS GROWTH
LEADERSHIP
COMMUNICATION
MEDIA & JOURNALISM
PERSONAL GROWTH
FAITH & PURPOSE
My Story My Purpose My Future
Ideas
I Create My Own Path
NE1 NEWS
✓ Confident
✓ Secure
✓ Purposeful
✓ Inspiring Others

Think About It...

What makes you unique? Think about your talents, your interests, or your personality.

Use these words to discover and describe who you are. Choose the ones that feel most like you.

unique	capable
confident	strong
authentic	proud
brave	worthy
creative	bold

____

____

____

____

____

____

Say Your 'I Am' Statement With Confidence And Own It.

I AM

"

You don't have to be like anyone else. Be yourself—because this world needs you to be you.

My
I AM
Page

Think about your journey through this book. What have you discovered about yourself?

____

____

____

____

____

In the space below, write several "I AM" statements that reflect your identity, your strengths, and who you are becoming.

Take your time. These statements matter.

____

____

____

____

____

My
Journal
Space

My Journal Space

What are three things you have learned about yourself from this book?

____

____

____

____

____

How do these things help you understand who you are?

____

____

____

____

____

My Journal Space

What are your strengths or talents?

How can you use them to help yourself and others?

My Journal Space

Think about a time when you faced a challenge or felt unsure of yourself.

____

____

____

____

What did you learn from that experience?

____

____

____

How did you grow?

____

____

____

My Journal Space

Describe a time when you made a good choice.

____

____

____

____

Why was that choice important?

____

____

____

What does this say about your character?

____

____

____

My Journal Space

My Journal Space

My Journal Space

My Journal Space

My Journal Space

My Journal Space

My Journal Space

A Final Message
to You

I am proud of you.

You completed this book, and that is something to be proud of. I hope that along the way, you learned more about yourself and began to think about the choices that shape who you are becoming.

Remember, growth doesn't stop here. Each day is a new opportunity to choose your thoughts, your actions, and the kind of person you want to be. Continue to build on what you've learned and choose to grow day by day. Encourage others around you to be the best version of themselves. Your words and actions can make a difference.

And even when it feels easier to follow the crowd, choose to be true to who you are. You were not created to be like everyone else.

You are unique—and that is more than okay. It is something to value.

Keep choosing. Keep growing. Keep being you.

Guide for Parents and Educators

Welcome

This book is designed to support learners as they reflect on their identity, choices, and personal growth. Through stories, reflection questions, and journal writing, readers are encouraged to think more deeply about who they are and who they are becoming.

While this book can be completed independently, your support can help deepen understanding, encourage meaningful conversations, and reinforce the lessons in everyday life.

Supporting the Reader

- Encourage the reader to move through the book at their own pace.

- Allow space for honest thinking and personal reflection.

- Ask open-ended questions that invite deeper conversation rather than focusing on "right" or "wrong" answers.

- Create a safe environment where thoughts and feelings can be shared freely.

Reflection and Journaling

- Encourage thoughtful responses in the journal sections.

- Remind the reader that their voice and perspective matter.

- Support them in making connections between the lessons in the book and their own experiences.

- Celebrate effort, honesty, and growth in their responses.

"I AM" Reflection Page

- Encourage the reader to take their time when writing their "I AM" statements.

- Ask them to explain why they chose certain statements and what those statements mean to them.

- Reinforce that identity is shaped through both understanding and daily choices.

- Remind them that their words have power and can help shape how they see themselves.

Talking About Each Chapter

Chapter 1 **A Moment in Gym Class:** Discuss confidence, self-awareness, and being open to trying new things.

Chapter 2 **Words That Stick:** Explore the impact of words and the importance of speaking with kindness and intention.

<table>
<tr><td>

Chapter 3</td><td>

I Watch and I Learn: Talk about learning from others and making thoughtful, positive choices.</td></tr>
<tr><td>

Chapter 4</td><td>

The People Who Show Up: Encourage gratitude and recognition of supportive people in their lives.</td></tr>
<tr><td>

Chapter 5</td><td>

Being Uniquely You!: Reinforce self-acceptance and the importance of embracing individuality.</td></tr>
</table>

Encouraging Growth Beyond the Book

- Model positive behaviors such as kindness, responsibility, and respect.

- Encourage the reader to make choices that reflect who they want to become.

- Highlight moments when they demonstrate confidence, integrity, and growth.

- Remind them that growth is a process that happens over time.

Closing

Thank you for supporting and encouraging this journey. Your presence, guidance, and conversations play an important role in helping learners grow in confidence, character, and self-awareness as they continue choosing who they are.

About the Author

Dr. Tache' Vereen is an author, speaker, and coach dedicated to helping individuals discover who they are, take ownership of their choices, and cultivate meaningful growth. As the founder of DOC with TV LLC and creator of The DOC Coaching Method™, she is passionate about empowering the next generation to walk confidently in their identity and purpose.